Songs for my King

A 31-Day Journey of Praise

Gerard Assey

Songs for my King:
A 31-Day Journey of Praise

By
Gerard Assey

Published by:
Gerard Assey
19/18, Palli Arasan Street
Anna Nagar East
Chennai - 600 102

ISBN: 978-81-989262-9-6

Table of Contents

Preface

Worship has always been at the heart of God's people. From the tabernacle of Moses to the songs of David, and from the early church to today's congregations, the people of God have lifted their voices in praise. The Psalms, in particular, remain our greatest guide, reminding us that worship is not just a ritual but a relationship — a response to who God is and what He has done.

This book, **'Songs for my King: *A 31-Day Journey of Praise*'**, has been written in that same spirit. It is a collection of psalm-like hymns, each inspired by Scripture, designed to direct our hearts, minds, and voices exclusively to the Lord. Every song is short and simple — about eight lines long — making them easy to remember, chant, or sing. They cover different themes of God's character: His majesty, mercy, greatness, faithfulness, righteousness, and more.

These daily songs can be used in different ways:

- ✓ ***Read** them devotionally as prayers of worship.*
- ✓ ***Sing** them by creating your own simple melody or chant.*

- ✓ ***Use*** *them in congregational worship, with the chorus repeated together by all.*

The goal is not performance but devotion. Whether read softly in personal prayer or sung aloud with a congregation, these songs allow us to return to the simplicity of worship that is both **scriptural and heartfelt**.

May this 31-day journey draw you closer to the heart of God, tune your spirit to His presence, and help you join the eternal song that will resound forever: *"To Him who sits on the throne and to the Lamb be blessing and honor and glory and might forever and ever!"* (Revelation 5:13).

How to Use This Book

This book is designed to guide you through a 31-day journey of daily worship using short, psalm-like hymns. Each day features one hymn, inspired by the Psalms and directed exclusively to God. Here are some practical ways you can use it:

For Individuals:

- ✓ ***Daily Devotion:*** *Read or sing one hymn each day during your quiet time, letting the words focus your heart on God.*
- ✓ ***Prayer Starter:*** *Use the hymn as an opening to your prayer, then continue speaking your own words of praise.*
- ✓ ***Scripture Meditation:*** *After each hymn, pause to reflect on the Scripture references provided, allowing God's Word to sink deeper into your heart.*
- ✓ ***Personal Melody:*** *Feel free to hum or create a simple tune that helps you remember and sing the words throughout the day.*

For Congregations:

- ✓ ***Opening Worship:*** *Begin services or gatherings with the day's hymn,* *allowing the whole congregation to declare it together.*

- ✓ ***Chorus Repetition:*** *Encourage everyone to repeat the short chorus line together, creating unity in praise.*
- ✓ ***Responsive Reading:*** *One leader can read the lines, and the congregation can respond with the chorus or the final line.*
- ✓ ***Teaching Tool:*** *Use the daily themes (e.g., Majesty of God, Faithfulness of God) to teach worship and theology through song.*

Flexibility:

These hymns are not tied to a fixed melody. You may:

- ✓ *Chant them slowly and reverently.*
- ✓ *Sing them freely with simple chords or instruments.*
- ✓ *Or adapt them into fuller songs as the Spirit leads.*

The aim is not musical perfection but heartfelt devotion. Whether alone or together, these daily songs will help anchor your life in praise, keeping God at the center of your day.

Day 1
Psalm of Majesty

O Lord, You are clothed with splendor bright,
The heavens declare Your power and might.

The earth bows low at Your mighty hand,
The stars bear witness at Your command.

Your voice resounds and creation sings,
The universe trembles before the King.

Your throne is forever, Your word is sure,
Your kingdom eternal shall ever endure.

(*Inspired by Psalm 104:1-2; Psalm 93:1)*

Chorus (repeat together):
"You reign forever, O King of glory… You reign forever our King!"

Day 2
Psalm of Thanksgiving

Great are Your works, O Lord Most High,
With songs of joy, Your praise we cry.

Your mercy endures through every age,
Your love is written on history's page.

You heal the broken, the lost You restore,
Your blessings abound, we can't count the store.

Our voices rise, Your wonders we tell,
You are our Refuge who does all things well.

(*Inspired by Psalm 107:1; Psalm 28:7)*

Chorus (repeat together):
"We bless Your name, our Strength and Shield!"

Day 3
Psalm of Adoration

Holy, holy, Lord of all,
Before Your throne the nations fall.

Your kingdom stands from age to age,
Your name is honored on every stage.

Your glory shines with radiant light,
The heavens proclaim Your power and might.

From dawn to dusk Your praises resound,
We worship in spirit, on holy ground.

(*Inspired by Psalm 99:5; Psalm 29:2)*

Chorus (repeat together):
"Holy are You, O Lord Most High!"

Day 4
Psalm of Joyful Praise

Sing to the Lord a song made new,
Clap your hands, all people too!

Rivers rejoice and mountains sing,
For endless love our praises bring.

The sun and moon in chorus reply,
The oceans roar with joyful cry.

The nations declare His mercies untold,
His faithfulness stands from days of old.

(*Inspired by Psalm 96:1; Psalm 98:8; Psalm 100:1-2)*

Chorus (repeat together):
"The Lord is good, His love forever!"

Day 5
Psalm of Exaltation

You are our Rock, Redeemer strong,
To You alone our hearts belong.

The heavens declare Your mighty name,
All creation Your glory proclaims.

The angels bow, the saints all adore,
Your greatness resounds forevermore.

From sunrise to sunset Your praise is due,
Forever we worship and honor You.

(*Inspired by Psalm 18:2; Psalm 19:1; Psalm 113:3)*

Chorus (repeat together):
"Glory and honor belong to You!"

Day 6
Psalm of God's Glory

The heavens declare Your glory above,
The skies proclaim Your power and love.

Day unto day pours forth Your praise,
Night unto night Your wonder displays.

No voice is heard, yet all men see,
Your glory revealed in majesty.

The earth is filled with works so grand,
All show the beauty of Your hand.

(*Inspired by Psalm 19:1-4; Psalm 72:19)*

Chorus (repeat together):
"Glory, glory to our God on high!"

Day 7
Psalm of God's Greatness

Great is the Lord, most worthy of praise,
His greatness shines through endless days.

The mountains tremble, the seas obey,
At His command they move or stay.

His works are mighty, His wisdom deep,
His promises faithful, His covenants keep.

No one can measure His boundless worth,
The Lord Most High, Creator of earth.

(*Inspired by Psalm 145:3-6; Psalm 95:3-5)*

Chorus (repeat together):
"Great are You, Lord, forever and ever!"

Day 8
Psalm of God's Faithfulness

Your faithfulness reaches the highest skies,
Your mercy flows where hope may die.

From age to age Your word is sure,
Your steadfast love shall long endure.

In darkest nights, You are my light,
A guiding lamp that shines so bright.

Forever true, both now and then,
The God of promise, faithful Amen.

(*Inspired by Psalm 36:5; Psalm 119:89-90; Psalm 100:5)*

Chorus (repeat together):
"Faithful forever, O Lord our God!"

Day 9
Psalm of the Power of His Word

Your word, O Lord, is tried and true,
A light to guide, a path made new.

Sharper than swords, it pierces the heart,
Life to the soul Your truths impart.

The grass may wither, the flowers fall,
But Your word endures and stands through all.

Sweeter than honey, pure and divine,
Your holy precepts forever shine.

(*Inspired by Psalm 119:105; Psalm 12:6; Psalm 19:7-10)*

Chorus (repeat together):
"Your word is life, eternal and strong!"

Day 10
Psalm of the Shepherd

The Lord is my Shepherd, I shall not lack,
He leads me forth on the righteous track.

In pastures green my soul finds rest,
By quiet waters my heart is blessed.

Though shadows fall, I will not fear,
Your rod and staff bring comfort near.

Goodness and mercy follow all days,
Forever I dwell in Your house of praise.

(*Inspired by Psalm 23:1-6)*

Chorus (repeat together):
"The Lord our Shepherd, forever we sing!"

Day 11
Psalm of Deliverance

You lift me up when troubles arise,
You hear my cry, You answer my sighs.

Chains are broken, the foe is slain,
Your mighty hand removes my pain.

You rescue the weak, the humble restore,
Your mercy abounds forevermore.

From pits of despair You set me free,
Deliverer strong, my song shall be!

(*Inspired by Psalm 18:2; Psalm 34:4,17*)

Chorus (repeat together):
"The Lord delivers, faithful and true!"

Day 12
Psalm of the Righteous Judge

Righteous and just are all Your ways,
The Judge of the earth deserves all praise.

You weigh the hearts, both great and small,
Your justice shines, impartial to all.

The wicked may boast, their power may stand,
But fall they will by Your mighty hand.

Your throne is founded on justice and right,
We worship the Judge who rules in light.

(*Inspired by Psalm 9:7-8; Psalm 96:10,13)*

Chorus (repeat together):
"Holy and righteous, O Lord, You reign!"

Day 13
Psalm of the Strong Tower

You are my fortress, my refuge secure,
A shelter of strength, steadfast and sure.

When storms arise, in You I hide,
In Your protection I safe abide.

The enemy flees, his schemes undone,
Your power defends, Your victory won.

O Rock of ages, my trust is in You,
A tower of safety, eternal and true.

(*Inspired by Psalm 61:3; Psalm 18:2)*

Chorus (repeat together):
"Our Strong Tower, we run to You!"

Day 14
Psalm of Light

The Lord is my light, whom shall I fear?
Your radiant presence draws ever near.

Darkness is banished, the night made day,
Your word illuminates every way.

Your face shines brighter than morning sun,
In You alone the victory's won.

O Light of the world, forever we sing,
You brighten our path, O radiant King.

(*Inspired by Psalm 27:1; Psalm 119:105)*

Chorus (repeat together):
"The Lord is my light, my joy, my song!"

Day 15
Psalm of the Eternal King

O King of glory, crowned on high,
Your throne is set above the sky.

The nations bow, the kings obey,
Your reign is forever, night and day.

From age to age Your kingdom stands,
Established by Your sovereign hands.

No end shall come to Your mighty reign,
Eternal King, forever remain!

(*Inspired by Psalm 24:7-10; Psalm 145:11-13)*

Chorus (repeat together):
"You reign forever, Eternal King!"

Day 16
Psalm of God's Holiness

Holy and pure are all Your ways,
Worthy of honor, worthy of praise.

No blemish, no shadow is found in You,
Faithful and righteous in all You do.

The seraphim cry, "Holy, the Lord!"
Heaven and earth in one accord.

We bow before Your throne so bright,
Worshipping You, O Lord of Light.

(*Inspired by Psalm 99:3,5,9)*

Chorus (repeat together):
"Holy, holy, holy is the Lord!"

Day 17
Psalm of God's Mercy

Merciful Lord, slow to be wrath,
Guiding the sinner to righteous path.

Your mercy is higher than mountain tall,
Your compassion extends to one and all.

Though we have failed, Your arms still embrace,
Covering us with amazing grace.

From age to age Your mercies flow,
Endless compassion Your people know.

(*Inspired by Psalm 103:8-12; Psalm 136:1*)

Chorus (repeat together):
"Your mercy endures forevermore!"

Day 18
Psalm of God's Wisdom

Your wisdom, Lord, no mind can contain,
Deeper than oceans, wider than plain.

You teach the humble, guide the meek,
Reveal Your truth to all who seek.

Your judgments stand both firm and sure,
Your counsel eternal shall endure.

O Lord of wisdom, perfect in might,
We walk by faith, not by sight.

(*Inspired by Psalm 104:24; Psalm 111:10; Psalm 119:98)*

Chorus (repeat together):
"O Lord of wisdom, guide us in truth!"

Day 19
Psalm of God's Protection

You are my shield, my hiding place,
Covered secure in Your embrace.

Arrows may fly and storms may rage,
Yet safe am I in every stage.

The snares are broken, the night made still,
I rest, O Lord, in Your perfect will.

No fear shall harm, no foe shall win,
For You are my fortress deep within.

(*Inspired by Psalm 3:3; Psalm 91:1-4)*

Chorus (repeat together):
"The Lord is my shield, my refuge strong!"

Day 20
Psalm of God's Nearness

The Lord is near to hearts that pray,
A present help by night or day.

Not far removed, nor distant King,
You dwell with us, Your praises we sing.

Closer than breath, Your Spirit abides,
Faithful Companion, always guides.

O God who hears, forever You stay,
Our Shepherd near, both night and day.

(*Inspired by Psalm 34:18; Psalm 145:18*)

Chorus (repeat together):
"The Lord is near, forever we sing!"

Day 21
Psalm of God's Holiness

O Lord, You shine in purity bright,
Clothed in splendor, robed in light.

No shadow dwells within Your Name,
Forever holy, always the same.

Angels cry "Holy!" with voices high,
We join their chorus, "Holy You reign on high!"

(*Inspired by Psalm 99:3,9)*

Chorus (Repeat):
"Holy, holy, holy, Lord God most high!"

Day 22
Psalm of God's Deliverance

You lift us up from pits of despair,
Setting our feet on ground most fair.

Chains are broken, fear has fled,
Your strong right hand our souls have led.

Through storm and battle, You make a way,
Deliverer forever, our song we say!

(*Inspired by Psalm 34:17–19*)

Chorus (Repeat):
"Our Deliverer lives, our Deliverer saves!"

Day 23
Psalm of God's Healing

You bind the wounds the world has torn,
You heal the heart that's weak and worn.

Your touch restores, Your Spirit mends,
Your mercy flows, Your power descends.

With joy renewed, our lips shall sing,
"Healer of nations, our mighty King!"

(*Inspired by Psalm 103:2–3)*

Chorus (Repeat):
"By His stripes we are healed, by His love we are sealed!"

Day 24
Psalm of God's Protection

A shield around, our refuge near,
Your presence drives away all fear.

The arrows fall, but not by night,
Your hand defends with holy might.

Beneath Your wings we safely hide,
In You, O Lord, we will abide.

(*Inspired by Psalm 91:1–4)*

Chorus (Repeat):
"Safe in His shadow, secure in His love."

Day 25
Psalm of God's Creation

The heavens proclaim Your glory bright,
The skies reveal Your endless might.

The seas resound, the mountains sing,
All earth declares its Maker King.

From dawn to dusk, Your works amaze,
Creation lifts its endless praise.

(*Inspired by Psalm 19:1–4*)

Chorus (Repeat):
"The heavens declare, the earth resounds—
Glory to our King!"

Day 26
Psalm of God's Mercy

Your mercy flows both deep and wide,
A river strong, our constant guide.

Though we have failed, Your grace remains,
Forgiveness triumphs, love sustains.

From age to age, Your mercies new,
O Lord of kindness, faithful and true.

(*Inspired by Psalm 136:1)*
Chorus (Repeat):
"Your mercy endures, forever secure!"

Day 27
Psalm of God's Wisdom

Your wisdom shines, more bright than gold,
A treasure rich, a truth untold.

You guide the path where we should go,
Your Word a lamp, Your light will show.

The fear of God, the wise man's start,
Your wisdom dwells within the heart.

(*Inspired by Psalm 111:10)*

Chorus (Repeat):
"Lord, teach us Your ways, Your wisdom we praise!"

Day 28
Psalm of God's Righteousness

Righteous and just are all Your ways,
Holy and pure through endless days.

No sin can stand, no wrong prevail,
Your truth endures, it shall not fail.

The righteous Judge, forever true,
All nations bow in awe of You.

(*Inspired by Psalm 11:7)*

Chorus (Repeat):
"Righteous and true are You, O Lord!"

Day 29
Psalm of God's Joy

You turn our mourning into song,
With joy that lifts our hearts along.

Your presence fills with holy cheer,
A strength that grows when You are near.

Eternal gladness You impart,
Your joy, O Lord, floods every heart.

(*Inspired by Psalm 16:11)*
Chorus (Repeat):
"The joy of the Lord is our strength forever!"

Day 30
Psalm of God's Justice

You break the chains the wicked bind,
Defend the poor, uphold the kind.

The hungry fed, the captive freed,
You act in truth, in every deed.

Your throne is built on what is right,
Justice and truth shine forth in light.

(*Inspired by Psalm 89:14*)

Chorus (Repeat):
"Justice and truth belong to the Lord!"

Day 31
Psalm of God's Eternity

From everlasting to ages unrolled,
Your years endure, Your power untold.

Before the mountains came to be,
You reigned in sovereign majesty.

Forevermore, our hearts will sing,
Eternal Lord, our timeless King!

(*Inspired by Psalm 90:1–2)*

Chorus (Repeat):
"From everlasting to everlasting—You are God!"

About the Author 'GERARD ASSEY'

Gerard Assey is a Graduate in Economics, a PGD in Management (HRD) and holds a Doctorate in Leadership. Gerard holds several International Qualifications in Sales, Debt Collection, Training & Teaching, and is a 'Fellow' of the prestigious 'Institute of Sales & Marketing Management'-UK, a Certified NLP Practitioner, a 'Certified Trainer', an 'Accredited Management Teacher-Behavioral Sciences', a 'Certified Competency Facilitator', a 'Certified Management Consultant'- (the International credentials of a professional management consultant, awarded in accordance with global standards of the ICMCI); and a Certification from the University of Michigan in 'Successful Negotiation: Essential Strategies and Skills'

He is also a Member of the 'National Association of Sales Professionals' backed with several years experience in varied industries, both in India and Overseas. He also holds an 'Etiquette Consultant' Certification from the USA (by Sue Fox, Author of Best Seller: 'Business Etiquette for Dummies'. She has trained some of the top celebrities' world over). He was also a recipient of a scholarship for extensive training in Japan on 'Corporate Management for India'.

Gerard Assey is 'Founder & Chief Corporate Trainer' of the Group: '**Citius, Altius, Fortius Unlimited**'- an organization that **celebrated 20 years of Glorious Service** in 2021, focusing on 3 Core Competencies:

People. Performance. Profit; in functional areas of Sales & Marketing, HR & Organizational Development, covering Recruitment, Training & Consultancy!

Having managed organizations with large Sales Forces in India & Overseas, his specialization cover extensive areas of Sales Training (All levels - Presentation, Negotiation, Key/ Strategic Accounts Management & Managerial Skills for all sectors), Bid Proposal/ Capture Planning/ Management Trainings, Retail Sales, Customer Service & Customer Retention Programs, Training for Prevention & Collection of Debt, Self & Personal Development Programs (Time Management, Teamwork & Team Building, Business Etiquette & Personal Grooming, Leadership & Managerial Skills, People Management Skills, Train-the-Trainer etc), including preparation of Custom-designed Business Manuals for Internal (HR, Induction, and Sales etc) & External use (Instruction, User Manuals).

Gerard has successfully conducted over 6480 Trainings & Workshops (as of Sept '25) all across India, Middle East, Africa, Europe & S.E. Asia. Besides public programs conducted regularly, both in India & Overseas, he has some of the top names as clients whom he services from Single Owners to large Public & Government undertakings, covering all sectors, for their in-house needs.

His website: www.CollectionSkills.com is the only one in this part of the world to be featured in the 'Collections & Credit Risk Magazine-USA' under 'Who's Who in Training' and ranks TOP, along with other websites listed below on most search engines.

Gerard is author of 206 Books already (Sept 2025), all the books being available on all online platforms and outlets as E-books and Paperbacks

A few of our business related books:

1. Bite-sized Bits on Commonsense Management
2. Heart to Heart on Life's Principles'
3. How to become a Successful Manager
4. The Sales Professionals' Master Workbook of S.Y.S.T.E.M.S
5. The Professional Business Email Etiquette Handbook & Guide
6. The Professional Business Video-Conferencing Etiquette Handbook & Guide
7. Professional Presentation Skills
8. Exceptional Customer Service
9. Professional Tele-Marketing Skills
10. Professional Debt Collection Skills
11. The G.R.E.A.T. Sales & Service Workbook
12. Sales Training Advantage for Results (*The Ultimate Sales Training Manual to enable you stand out as a S.T.A.R.*)
13. CEO Daily Planner & Organizer
14. The Sales Professionals' Master Daily Planner
15. The Professional Debt Collector's Master Daily Planner
16. My Daily Planner & Organizer
17. MY EMERGENCY INFORMATION RECORD (Family Emergency & Peace of Mind Planner)
18. The Ultimate Therapist & Counselors Planner and Organizer
19. Building an Ethical Workplace
20. Managing Relationships at Work
21. Managing Business Meetings Effectively
22. Effective Delegation Skills
23. Goal Setting for Success
24. B2B Selling by Email
25. Professional Business Etiquette & Grooming
26. Dining Etiquette & Table Manners
27. Effective Networking Skills
28. Grooming, Etiquette & Manners for Teens, Young Adults & Future Leaders
29. Inter-Personal Skills
30. Get Ready, Get Hired!
31. Selling in a Recession
32. Effective Receivables Management in an Economic Downturn!
33. Real Estate & Property Sales Training
34. Credit Sales & Accounts Receivable Management

35. Selling Skills for Real Estate & Property Advisors
36. Take G.R.E.A.T. C.A.R.E!
37. Spa, Salon & Health Club Selling Skills
38. Selling Travel, Holiday & MICE Services
39. Selling Skills for Spa's, Salons & Health Clubs
40. Retailing in Salons & Spas
41. Selling Holiday, Vacation, Tours & Packages
42. The Power of Sales Referrals
43. Selling Luxury
44. Technical Selling Skills
45. Financial Advisors Sales Training
46. Dealing with Burnout at Work Monopolize Your Markets
47. Selling to Affluent Customers
48. Growing up with Grace
49. Financial Selling Skills
50. *The Effective Manager's Guide: Key Skills to Thrive*
51. From Aspiring to Inspiring: A Guide for New Managers on the Rise
52. The Power of Focus
53. Selling with Integrity: Sell Like Jesus The Perfect Role Model!
54. 31 Habits of Champions: Your 31-Day Journey to Greatness
55. Rejecting Grasshopper Talk: From Grasshopper to Giant-Killer-*Defeating Giants Daily!*
56. Navigate the AI-Powered Future of Bid & Proposals: Up-Skill to Stay Relevant with Alternative Career Paths & Opportunities
57. Hiring Sales Winners
58. Present with Impact
59. Success Unlocked: *Breaking Free from Habits that Hold You Back*
60. Complaints to Cheers, Feedback to Gold: Mastering Complaints Management
61. Thriving Together: *Cultivating Diversity, Equity, and Inclusion*
62. Coaching Skills for Sales Managers
63. Soaring to Success in Business & Leadership: Swifter, Higher, Stronger!
64. From Classroom to Podium: A Student's Guide to Powerful Public Speaking & Presentation Skills
65. Developing Self-Discipline
66. The CEO's 31-Day Power Plan: Unlocking Success through Essential Traits

67. Credibility Matters
68. A Winning Attitude
69. Bid & Proposal Management Using AI
70. Sales Forecasting: A Practical & Proven Guide to Strategic Sales Forecasting
71. Elevate & Energize: *50 Dynamic & Fun Activities for Peak Workplace Morale*
72. 'Sales SOS! Sales on Fire! *30 Days to Conquer Chaos & the Nightmares of Success!'*
73. Mastering Sales Managerial Skills: *Building High-Performing Teams & Driving Exceptional Results*
74. Eagle-Eyed Leadership: Unleashing the Power of 31 Lessons from Eagles
75. The Ultimate Employee Training Guide: *Training Today, Leading Tomorrow*
76. Being More Accountable at Work
77. Creating a Culture of Continuous Improvement
78. Effective Questioning & Listening Skills
79. The Power of Value Selling
80. The Growth Mindset
81. Mastering Professional Help Desk Skills
82. The Power to Lead with Empathy
83. Being Prepared: The Key to Unlocking Success
84. Youthful Spark-Youth Energizers, Activities and Games-Igniting the Fun in Youth
85. Ignite your Motivation for Success
86. Elevate Your Executive Presence: *Your Roadmap to Executive Excellence*
87. Smart Decisions: *Mastering Problem Solving with Strategic Solutions for Business Success*
88. Strategic Planning: *Developing and Implementing Strategic Plans to Achieve Long-Term Business Goals*
89. The Power of Stay Interviews
90. Developing G.R.I.T.
91. Adaptability
92. Diagnosis- *A Key Skill for Leadership*
93. The Burnout-Proof Salesperson: *The Master Guide to Preventing Stress & Burnout-* Strategies for Thriving in Sales
94. Learning from Failure: *Keys to Success*
95. Customer Success Management
96. Overcoming the Killers of Motivation
97. The C-Suite Code: *Mastering Skills for Executive Excellence'*

98. Dealing with Difficult Customers
99. Unlocking Your Potential: Mastering the Top 20 Life Skills for a Brighter Future
100. Nurturing Tomorrow's Leaders: *Essential Soft Skills Every Child Must Learn*
101. Lively & Fun Party Games for Seniors & Elders
102. Role Playing for Sales Champions: From Practice to Performance
103. Fun and Exciting Party Games for Kids
104. Case Studies for Sales
105. Role-Playing for Unbeatable Customer Service
106. Case Studies in Customer Service
107. Case Studies in Winning Negotiations
108. Case Studies in Management & Leadership
109. Case Studies in Human Resources & Talent Management
110. CEO Success Blueprint: The Essential Toolkit for CEOs and C-Level Executives
111. The Salesperson's Self-Coaching Guide: *Master Your Own Self-Coaching Plan for Success*
112. Overcoming Procrastination: *Your Ultimate Guide to Stop Delaying and Start Living Your Best Life*
113. When True Colors Are Exposed: *The Journey to Unmasking Humanity*
114. Life-Changing Habits for Teens: Teen Success Blueprint for a Bright Future
115. Workplace Stress-Free: *Proven Strategies to Thrive at Work and Beyond*
116. Objection Overruled: *The Ultimate Guide to Turning 'No' into 'Yes'*
117. Building Strong Teams: *A Comprehensive Guide to Team Building*
118. Ethical & Moral Leadership in Business: *Eliminating Unethical Practices & Building a Culture of Trust & Integrity*
119. Rising Strong: Building Positive: High Self-Esteem for a Fulfilling Life-*A Practical Guide for Students, Employees, Leaders & Entrepreneurs*
120 The Cheerful Mindset: Cultivating a Joyful Outlook Everyday
121. Leading Through Crisis: Case Studies on Crisis Management

From the Ministry side, Gerard graduated in the very first batch of Charis Bible College-India & had for over 9 years served as a Part-time Faculty at Charis Bible College-Chennai (Andrew Wommack Ministries-Colorado, USA).
He also holds a Diploma in Worship (a subject closest to his heart) from the JSOW and is also a graduate of the Advanced Mentorship Program (AMP) and the Circle Of Ministerial Engagement (C.O.M.E.) of Prophet Jerome Fernando and a Spiritual Son of the Esteemed Prophet.
An accomplished author of several Secular & Christian Books, Gerard has been on the board of a few international organizations and boasts of being the SON of the MOST HIGH GOD: An ordinary guy following an extraordinary GOD!

...And some of his most recent Christian Books being:

1. A Bouquet of Praises for My KING
2. Christian Jokes for the Serious Religious' Folks!
3. Jesus Healed You!
4. Praise24Ever! (also in Tamil version)
5. The 5G Network of GOD
6. Building Faith over F.E.A.R- FACE EVERYTHING AND RISE with JESUS
7. Hebrew and Greek Praise and Worship Words
8. Godly Mothers' and Grandmothers' Bible Story time for Kids!
9. Miracles of Jesus in Pictures
10. Raise your Praise all 365 Days
11. Thanking GOD with an Attitude of Gratitude
12. Meditating on the Attributes of GOD
13. Puppet Scripts
14. Alcohol Ruins, JESUS Reforms, Renews & Restores!
15. Habakkuk 2:2 Christian Daily Journal, Planner & Organizer
16. ABC of GOD's Word for Handwriting Practice
17. Daily Bible Verse Handwriting Practice (Building Godly Character & Faith through Cursive Handwriting Practice!)
18. Guiding Light: Fun & Faith-Building Bible Activities for Children
19. Rejecting Grasshopper Talk: From Grasshopper to Giant-Killer-*Defeating Giants Daily!*
20. Teen Titans of Faith: *Building Courage, Determination & Christ-like-Esteem*
21. I AM Empowered: *Unleashing Divine Power with Positive*

Declarations

22. Be A Solution Provider-*From Passion to Purpose*: *A Biblical Guide to Being the Answer to the World!*
23. Miracles of JESUS
24. Parables of Jesus for a Meaningful Life!
25. A Grateful Heart: Importance of Sharing Testimonies of GOD's Grace
26. Melodies of Worship to JESUS: 31 Songs of Praise & Worship From My Heart to HIS!
27. I AM SO BLESSED!
28. My Daily Cup of Energizer
29. 31 Leadership Lessons *from* Jesus- *The Supreme Leader*
30. Peace Amidst Storms: A Biblical Guide to Conquering S.T.R.E.S.S.
31. Rise Above: 20 Biblical Eagle Lessons for Life's Triumphs
32. Godly Goal Setting: *The FAITHFUL Blueprint for a Purpose-Driven Life*
33. The Profound Attributes of our Mighty GOD: Understanding the 10S's of the Almighty
34. Worship Now, Worship Forever: *A Journey from Earthly Praise to Eternal Glory*
35. Unceasing Praise & Worship: *365 Days to Worship the King*
36. The ROAR Within: *Living with Purpose and Authority through the Power of the Holy Spirit*
37. From Potential to Purpose: Unlocking and Multiplying Your Talents & Gifts for Kingdom Impact
38. Songs from the Heart: *Worshipping GOD in Your Own Tune & Melody*
39. Awakening Praise & Worship: Hebrew & Greek Words to Raise Your Praise
40. Sing a NEW Song to the LORD Everyday: *Daily Devotions of Praise & Worship to Lift Your Heart & Glorify HIS Name*
41. *The* A.R.O.M.A. of True Worship: *Creating Worship That Delights God*
42. Becoming A Kingdom Champion: *Embracing God's Call for a Life of Purpose & Victory*
43. The Busy Businessman's Daily Devotional: 366 Crisp Truths to Start Your Day Strong
44. The Teacher's Heart: *Daily Devotions for Educators*
45. Anchored! *A 31-Day Devotional for Students Facing Life's Challenges*
46. Suddenly! Unlocking Unorthodox Breakthroughs through Unusual Worship

47. Overcoming Adversity: *Lessons from the Bible for Modern Challenges*
48. LORD, Don't do it without me
49. Kingdom Leadership: *Biblical Principles for Modern Leaders*
50. Heartprints of God- *Growing God's Way:* Daily Devotions for Kids to Shine Bright
51. Send Judah First: Let your Praises Go up First to See the Mighty Move of GOD
52. DIVINE MOMENTS: *Recognizing, Embracing, Preparing, and Walking into Life-Changing Encounters with God*
53. Be a Builder in the Kingdom: *The C.E.M.E.N.T. Guide to Creating a Lasting Legacy*
54. Unshakable: *Pillars of Godly Womanhood* (Pillars of Faith That Changed History)
55. Lead Like a Shepherd: *14 Essential Traits for Pastoral Excellence*
56. The Worship Leader's Arsenal: *Powerful Exhortations to Ignite Thanksgiving, Praise & Worship*
57. Women of UnShakable Faith: *31-Day Devotional for Strength, Purpose & Influence*
58. Called to Teach: *A Complete 10-Week Training Guide for Impactful VBS Teachers*
59. Strumming for the KING: Cowboy Songs of Faith & Fire
60. The Ultimate Youth Camp Playbook: *50 Bible-Centered Indoor Games to Engage, Equip, and Empower Teens*
61. Glad in HIS Presence: *David's Revelation of GOD's Love & Mercy*
62. The Spirit Behind the Sound: *52 Devotionals for Worship Teams*
63. THE COWBOY'S COMPASS: *Riding the Trail of Faith with Grit & Grace*
64. Worship as My Weapon: *Living Victoriously through the Power of Praise*
65. A Worshipper Always Wins*: Living a Life of Victorious Worship*
66. Worship That Leads to the Throne: *Practical Strategies for Worship Leaders to Inspire Their Team & Usher People into God's Presence*
67. Worship as Warfare: *Conquering through the Sound of Surrender*
68. Watchmen on the Walls: *A 31-Day Devotional for Worship Teams*

69. KINGDOM BUSINESS: *52 Biblical Principles for GODLY Leadership & Wise Decisions*
70. From Evening to Morning: *Rediscovering GOD's Sacred Hours*
71. Waves of Glory: *Worship through Dance, Flags, Staff & Sound*
72. WORSHIP TEAM BUILDER: *Guiding Your Team from Formation to Fruitfulness*
73. The Worship Leader's Master Training Manual
74. Skits for the King: Children's Plays for Every Church Occasion
75. Unbreakable: Building Strong Marriages and Families God's Way *(From Vows to Victory)*
76. Songs for my King: *A 31-Day Journey of Praise*

Besides regularly contributing to business & trade journals, including international ones such as the 'Creative Training Techniques' and the 'Sales News' of the U.S.A, He is also a member of several prestigious bodies & trade associations, having participated in many Conferences & Workshops in India & Overseas.
Prior to his last assignment of leading & managing a large MNC as head, Gerard had a 3-year stint in the Middle East as a Consultant with a leading British Consultancy Firm.

As the past 'Official Country Representative' for the International Business Award- 'THE STEVIES'-(the business world's own Oscar) for about 4 years- he ensured a few Indian companies that qualify for the same every year!

Gerard can be contacted at:

Email: training@Sales-Training.in,training@CollectionSkills.com
Websites:

- www.Sales-Training.in
- www.EtiquetteWorks.in
- www.CollectionSkills.com
- www.RetailSalesTraining.in
- www.SalesTrainingIndia.com
- www.ManualPreparation.com
- www.TrainingWithPuppets.com
- www.FirstContactAcademy.com
- www.SalesAndMarketingRecruiter.com

www.ingramcontent.com/pod-product-compliance
Ingram Content Group UK Ltd.
Pitfield, Milton Keynes, MK11 3LW, UK
UKHW020050200726
13845UKWH00055B/677

9 788198 926296